J 599.53 PRE   GC

PREVOST, JOHN F.
SPOTTED DOLPHINS

GARFIELD COUNTY LIBRARIES
Carbondale Branch Library
320 Sopris Ave
Carbondale, CO 81623
(970) 963-2889 – Fax (970) 963-8573
www.gcpld.org

D0819848

GORDON COOPER BRANCH LIBRARY
Phone: 970-963-2889
76 South 4th Street
Carbondale, CO 81623

DOLPHINS

SPOTTED DOLPHINS

JOHN F. PREVOST
ABDO & Daughters

Published by Abdo & Daughters, 4940 Viking Drive, Suite 622, Edina, Minnesota 55435.

Library bound edition distributed by Rockbottom Books, Pentagon Tower, P.O. Box 36036, Minneapolis, Minnesota 55435.

Copyright © 1996 by Abdo Consulting Group, Inc., Pentagon Tower, P.O. Box 36036, Minneapolis, Minnesota 55435 USA. International copyrights reserved in all countries. No part of this book may be reproduced in any form without written permission from the publisher.

Printed in the United States.

Cover Photo credit: Peter Arnold, Inc.
Interior Photo credits: Peter Arnold, Inc.

Edited by Bob Italia

Library of Congress Cataloging-in-Publication Data

Prevost, John F.
    Spotted dolphins / by John F. Prevost.
        p.   cm. — (Dolphins)
Includes bibliographical references and index.
    ISBN 1-56239-495-9
1. Stenella—Juvenile literature. [1. Spotted dolphins. 2. Dolphins.] I. Title. II. Series:
Prevost, John F.   Dolphins.
QL737.C432P7455   1995
599.5'3—dc20   95-12365
                                                                                CIP
                                                                                AC

ABOUT THE AUTHOR
John Prevost is a marine biologist and diver who has been active in conservation and education issues for the past 18 years. Currently he is living inland and remains actively involved in freshwater and marine husbandry, conservation and education projects.

Contents

SPOTTED DOLPHINS AND FAMILY

Spotted dolphins live in **tropical** and warm-**temperate** waters of the Atlantic and Pacific oceans. Dolphins are small-toothed whales. Whales are **mammals**. Like humans, they are **warm blooded**, breathe air with lungs, and make milk for their babies.

Many scientists believe there are only two spotted dolphin **species**. The spotted dolphin is also known as the bridled and white-dotted dolphin. Relatives of the spotted dolphin are the spinner and striped dolphins.

The spotted dolphin is also known as the bridled and white-dotted dolphin.

SIZE, SHAPE AND COLOR

Spotted dolphins are 6 to 8 feet (1.9 to 2.5 meters) in length. Males are slightly larger than females.

There are several different spotted dolphin groups. All have streamlined bodies and long snouts. **Coastal** spotted dolphins have heavier bodies. Offshore groups have more streamlined bodies.

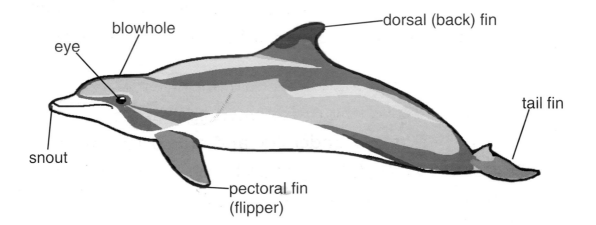

eye

blowhole

dorsal (back) fin

tail fin

snout

pectoral fin
(flipper)

Spotted dolphins get their name from their body spots.

Spotted dolphin groups also have their own colors. Some are a blue-gray color with small light spots. Other dolphins have a lighter underside and are covered with light and dark spots. A few groups have stripes on their sides and flippers. The sizes, shapes and colors make it hard to tell spotted dolphins apart.

WHERE THEY LIVE

Spotted dolphins are found throughout **tropical** and warm-**temperate** waters in the Atlantic and Pacific oceans. There are at least 2 different **species** with several different groups. They are found along coasts and offshore.

The **coastal** groups live in shallow water and **migrate** offshore for the winter. These dolphins form **pods** of up to 100 members. The average pod size is 50.

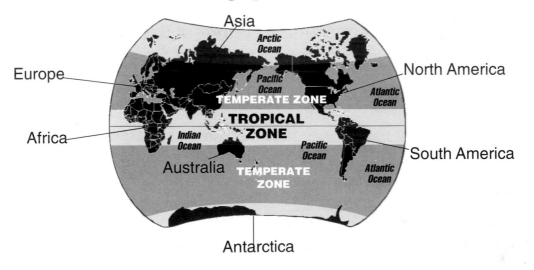

Spotted dolphins are found throughout tropical and warm-temperate waters in the Atlantic and Pacific oceans.

Offshore groups live in deep water and travel in search of food. They may form **pods** of up to 4,000 members for **migration**. But pods of 100 are more common.

Spotted dolphins often swim with other dolphin **species**. In the Pacific, they swim with yellowfin tuna.

SENSES

Spotted dolphins and people have 4 of the same senses. Their eyesight is good. They can see well in or out of the water. Spotted dolphins will often leap above the water to look around.

Hearing is their most important sense. Toothed whales have **echolocation**. By sending out a series of whistles, these animals can "see" underwater by listening to returning echoes.

Spotted dolphins are **social** animals. They often touch each other to **communicate**. Dolphins have a sense of taste, but lack the sense of smell.

HOW ECHOLOCATION WORKS

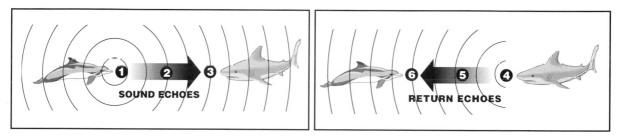

The dolphin sends out sound echoes (1). These echoes travel in all directions through the water (2). The sound echoes reach an object in the dolphin's path (3), then bounce off it (4). The return echoes travel through the water (5) and reach the dolphin (6). These echoes let the dolphin know where the object is, how large it is, and how fast it is moving.

Spotted dolphins are social animals that often touch each other to communicate.

DEFENSE

Spotted dolphins have few **predators**: large sharks, killer whales and man. Speed and quickness are their best defense. Their well-developed sense of hearing allows the **pods** to listen for danger and **communicate** warnings. Young dolphins and weak adults are the most likely **prey**.

In the Pacific, groups that swim with yellowfin tuna are often trapped in tuna nets. New laws and equipment have lowered the numbers of dolphins injured and killed in these nets.

Its well-developed sense of hearing allows the spotted dolphin to listen for danger and communicate warnings.

FOOD

Spotted dolphins **prey** on small fish and **squid** near the surface. They have 34 to 45 pairs of teeth in each jaw. Their teeth are made to grab prey, not cut or chew. So the prey they eat is swallowed whole.

Spotted dolphins work together to find and catch food. They combine these activities with loud whistles that can be heard long distances underwater. They also use **echolocation** to find their food.

Spotted dolphins prey on small fish and squid near the surface.

BABIES

A baby spotted dolphin is called a **calf**. At birth, a calf is 31 to 36 inches (79 to 91 centimeters) long. Like other **mammals,** the mother makes milk for the calf.

Spotted dolphins are **social** animals. Females in the **pod** will assist the mother by "baby-sitting" the calf while the mother is feeding. This helps them to safely raise their calves. Calves **nurse** for at least a year.

Spotted dolphins, mother and calf.

SPOTTED DOLPHIN FACTS

Scientific Name: *Stenella attenuata*
S. dubia
S. frontalis
S. plagiodon

Average Size: 6 to 8 feet (1.9 to 2.5 meters).
Males are often larger than
females.

Where They're Found: In **tropical** and warm-**temperate**
regions in the Atlantic and
Pacific oceans.

The spotted dolphin.

GLOSSARY

CALF - A baby dolphin.

COASTAL - Bordering on water, shore.

COMMUNICATE (kuh-MEW-nih-kate) - To exchange or share feelings.

ECHOLOCATION (ek-oh-low-KAY-shun) - The use of sound waves to find objects underwater.

MAMMAL - A group of animals, including humans, that have hair and feed their young milk.

MIGRATE - To pass periodically from place to place repeatedly.

NURSE - To feed a child or young animal from its mother's breasts.

POD - A herd or school of sea mammals.

PREDATOR (PRED-uh-tor) - An animal that eats other animals.

PREY - Animals that are eaten by other animals.

SOCIAL - To live in organized groups.

SPECIES (SPEE-seas) - A group of related living things that have common traits.

SQUID - Sea animals related to the octopus that are streamlined and have at least ten arms.

TEMPERATE (TEM-prit) - Moderate to cool water located between the polar and tropical waters.

TROPICAL (TRAH-pih-kull) - The part of the Earth near the equator where the oceans are very warm.

WARM-BLOODED - An animal whose body temperature remains the same and warmer than the outside air or water temperature.

Index

BIBLIOGRAPHY

Cousteau, Jacques-Yves. *The Whale, Mighty Monarch of the Sea.* N.Y.: Doubleday, 1972.

Dozier, Thomas A. *Whales and other Sea Mammals.* Time-Life Films, 1977.

Leatherwood, Stephen. *The Sierra Club Handbook of Whales and Dolphins.* San Francisco, California: Sierra Club Books, 1983.

Minasian, Stanley M. *The World's Whales.* Washington, D.C.: Smithsonian Books, 1984.

Ridgway, Sam H., ed. *Mammals of the Sea.* Springfield, Illinois: Charles C. Thomas Publisher, 1972.